W9-AVJ-803

NUTRITION AND
YOUR BODY

YOUR
BODY ON
CAFFEINE

BY MARCIA AMIDON LUSTED

CONTENT CONSULTANT
Leah M. Panek-Shirley, PhD
Assistant Professor, Health, Nutrition, and Dietetics
Buffalo State College

Cover image: Many coffee drinks, including iced,
blended coffees, have caffeine.

Core Library

An Imprint of Abdo Publishing
abdobooks.com

abdocorelibrary.com

Published by Abdo Publishing, a division of ABDO, PO Box 398166,
Minneapolis, Minnesota 55439. Copyright © 2020 by Abdo Consulting
Group, Inc. International copyrights reserved in all countries. No part of this
book may be reproduced in any form without written permission from the
publisher. Core Library™ is a trademark and logo of Abdo Publishing.

Printed in the United States of America, North Mankato, Minnesota
022019
092019

**THIS BOOK CONTAINS
RECYCLED MATERIALS**

Cover Photo: Shutterstock Images
Interior Photos: Shutterstock Images, 1, 16, 21 (paraxanthine), 21 (adenosine), 25, 31 (beverages),
37; Joshua Resnick/Shutterstock Images, 4–5; Olena Yakobchuk/Shutterstock Images, 6;
iStockphoto, 10–11, 18–19, 26–27, 29, 43, 45; Shulevskyy Volodymyr/Shutterstock Images, 12–13;
Mironova Iuliia/Shutterstock Images, 31 (chocolates); Allan Cash Picture Library/Alamy, 34–35;
Wilfredo Lee/AP Images, 40

Editor: Marie Pearson
Series Designer: Claire Vanden Branden

Library of Congress Control Number: 2018965967

Publisher's Cataloging-in-Publication Data

Names: Lusted, Marcia Amidon, author.
Title: Your body on caffeine / by Marcia Amidon Lusted
Description: Minneapolis, Minnesota: Abdo Publishing, 2020 | Series: Nutrition and your body |
    Includes online resources and index.
Identifiers: ISBN 9781532118821 (lib. bdg.) | ISBN 9781532173004 (ebook) | ISBN
    9781644940730 (pbk.)
Subjects: LCSH: Caffeine--Physiological effect--Juvenile literature. | Caffeine habit--Juvenile
    literature. | Food--Health aspects--Juvenile literature.
Classification: DDC 613.20--dc23

CONTENTS

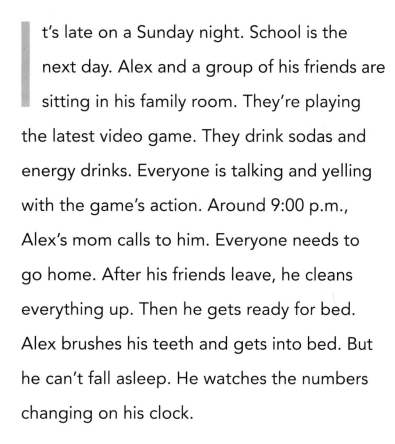

LATE NIGHTS WITH CAFFEINE

It's late on a Sunday night. School is the next day. Alex and a group of his friends are sitting in his family room. They're playing the latest video game. They drink sodas and energy drinks. Everyone is talking and yelling with the game's action. Around 9:00 p.m., Alex's mom calls to him. Everyone needs to go home. After his friends leave, he cleans everything up. Then he gets ready for bed. Alex brushes his teeth and gets into bed. But he can't fall asleep. He watches the numbers changing on his clock.

Alex tosses and turns. He punches his pillow and tries to relax. But his mind

Some people do not realize that sodas can contain caffeine.

Many people rely on a morning cup of coffee to wake them up for the day.

is whirling. Soon it's midnight. He's still wide awake. How many sodas and energy drinks did he have? He can't even remember.

INSIDE THE BODY

Caffeine is a drug. It's the most widely used drug in the world. Most people think of it as being in coffee. But it's also in tea, chocolate, and energy drinks. And it's in unexpected places. It may be affecting people in ways they don't know about.

Alex didn't know how caffeine works inside his body. It began with the first sip Alex took of that first energy drink. His body started absorbing the caffeine in the drink. It traveled through the membranes lining his mouth, throat, and stomach. His liver broke down the caffeine. In just 45 minutes, 99 percent of the caffeine reached Alex's bloodstream. The caffeine will stay in his body for four to six hours.

The caffeine is coursing through

DISCOVERING COFFEE

An Ethiopian legend tells how coffee was discovered. A goatherder named Kaldi was watching his goats. The goats ate red berries from a bush. The bush was the coffee shrub. The goats became energetic. Kaldi tried the fruit. He became more energetic too. He shared his story with others. Coffee became popular.

BEFORE THE COFFEE DRINK

Coffee is made from coffee beans. But they aren't actually beans. They are the pits inside coffee shrub berries. People did not start making coffee beans into a hot drink until the 1200s CE. Before then, some people mixed the ripe berries with animal fat. This made a kind of protein bar. Sometimes they made the berries into a drink like wine. Later, they roasted coffee beans. They did this to see if the beans would become less bitter. Then they boiled the beans to make them softer. The result was something like today's coffee.

Alex's blood. The blood carries it through the body and brain. This makes Alex feel awake and happy. It also keeps him from sleeping. Because of the caffeine, his body ignores the usual signals that make him sleepy.

THE AFTERMATH

The chemicals that caffeine releases into the body don't stay forever. They will eventually leave the body during urination. Then Alex's brain can do what it was supposed to do hours ago. It makes Alex sleepy. The chemicals that flooded

Alex's body with energy have left. Now he feels tired. This tiredness is called withdrawal. Alex's alarm wakes him up the next morning. He is already tired. So when he gets to school, he grabs a cup of coffee from the cafeteria. The caffeine soon enters his bloodstream. The whole process starts again.

EXPLORE ONLINE

Chapter One talks about the effects of caffeine in the body. The website below also gives information about caffeine and its effects. Does the article support the descriptions of what happens to Alex when he drinks too much caffeine? What additional information does it have?

KIDSHEALTH: CAFFEINE
abdocorelibrary.com/caffeine

IT'S EVERYWHERE!

Some people think caffeine is only found in coffee. But caffeine is in many kinds of foods. It is a natural part of some foods. These include coffee beans and tea leaves. Kola nuts were originally used to make cola-flavored sodas. A single nut contains as much caffeine as two cups of brewed coffee. Cacao beans are used to make chocolate. They also naturally have caffeine. People discovered a long time ago that foods with caffeine could perk them up.

CAFFEINE'S POPULARITY

People use plants with caffeine to make many foods and drinks. Those foods and drinks end

Cacao beans are made into a powder that is used to make many chocolate products.

Different kinds of tea have different levels of caffeine. Black tea tends to have the most caffeine.

up with caffeine too. Caffeine is commonly found in coffee drinks. It is in many sodas. It's in tea and energy drinks. Some energy and protein bars also have caffeine.

Cacao beans are used to make chocolate. That means chocolate candy has caffeine. The darker the

chocolate, the more caffeine it has. Some candy manufacturers add extra caffeine to their chocolate. Hot cocoa contains caffeine. So do coffee- and mocha-flavored ice creams. Even puddings, breakfast cereals, and frozen yogurt can have caffeine. These foods can contain caffeine if they have chocolate flavors.

WHAT DOES CAFFEINE DO?

Caffeine's popularity is partially due to the fact that it is a drug. It is a type of drug called a stimulant. Stimulants are substances that stimulate the brain and the central nervous system. They usually make people feel alert, happy, and energetic. Caffeine is a mild stimulant. People have used it for centuries. But some stimulants are very strong. These include nicotine, found in tobacco. Cocaine is one of the most powerful stimulants. Nicotine and cocaine are dangerous. People easily become addicted

KOLA IN MY COLA?

Kola nuts are about the size of chestnuts. They taste bitter when fresh. When dried and chewed, they have a mild taste. They smell like nutmeg. Originally, kola nuts were used to make cola-flavored sodas such as Coca-Cola. Today, some soda manufacturers use kola nut extract. Others use a chemical combination of flavorings that tastes like kola nuts.

to them. Both can cause severe health issues. Laws limit their use.

Caffeine is a stimulant that's easy to get. It's legal. It's in foods people eat daily. It can also be addictive. Some people drink a certain amount of coffee or tea every morning. They will often feel tired and get headaches if they don't have as much caffeine. People use caffeine to make themselves feel more awake and to fight tiredness. It can also help them focus.

CAFFEINE AND PETS

Caffeine can be a big problem for pets including dogs and cats. They are more sensitive to caffeine than humans. Even a little caffeine can harm them. A cat or dog may eat chocolate or foods with chocolate flavoring. A 15-pound (7-kg) dog only has to eat 3 or 4 ounces (85–113 g) of dark chocolate to get very sick. Pets experience increased heart rates and hyperactivity. They may start to shake. In extreme cases, they can die from too much caffeine.

Cigarettes have nicotine, which is addictive, making it hard for people to quit smoking, even if they want to.

Most people consume caffeine. They don't really think about it unless it causes them to have a sleepless night. But a lot happens in the body when someone consumes caffeine.

STRAIGHT TO THE
SOURCE

In a 2018 interview, American Cancer Society researchers Susan Gapstur and Marjorie McCullough explained some of the potential health benefits of coffee:

> *Recent studies find that coffee may lower the risk of several types of cancer . . . although the potential beneficial effects of coffee are not completely understood. . . . Caffeine . . . and other coffee compounds have been shown to increase energy expenditure, inhibit cellular damage, regulate genes involved in DNA repair, have anti-inflammatory properties and/or inhibit metastasis [spread of cancer], among other activities. There is also evidence that coffee consumption is associated with lower risk of insulin resistance and type 2 diabetes.*

Source: Elizabeth Mendes. "Coffee and Cancer: What the Research Really Shows." *American Cancer Society*. American Cancer Society, April 3, 2018. Web. Accessed October 23, 2018.

Back It Up

The author of this passage is using evidence to support a point. Write a paragraph describing the point the author is making. Then write down two or three pieces of evidence the author uses to make the point.

CHAPTER
THREE

YOUR BRAIN ON CAFFEINE

Caffeine enters the body in foods, beverages, supplements, and medicines. The small intestine absorbs it. From there, it makes its way into the bloodstream. Then it travels to the liver. The liver breaks it down into three chemicals. These chemicals are theophylline, theobromine, and paraxanthine.

A TRIP THROUGH THE BODY

The small intestine moves these chemicals into the blood. The blood carries them through the entire body. The chemicals affect different functions. Theophylline relaxes certain muscles in the body, including those in the colon.

The digestive system breaks down food and beverages into nutrients the body can use.

This can make people need to use the bathroom more often. Theobromine also increases the amount of urine the body makes. Paraxanthine also makes its way into the brain. It is attracted to a set of receptors there. These receptors usually attract a molecule called adenosine. Adenosine is what tells the body that it's time to sleep.

Paraxanthine takes the place of adenosine on these receptors. It blocks the effects of adenosine. Without adenosine, the brain cells work faster. The body responds to the hyperactive brain cells as if there were an emergency. The body produces epinephrine. Epinephrine is sometimes called adrenaline. Epinephrine makes the body feel alert and energetic. In an emergency, this would help the person escape danger.

At the same time, paraxanthine wakes up the dopamine system in the brain. Dopamine is a neurotransmitter. Neurotransmitters are chemicals that allow messages to be sent between cells. Dopamine

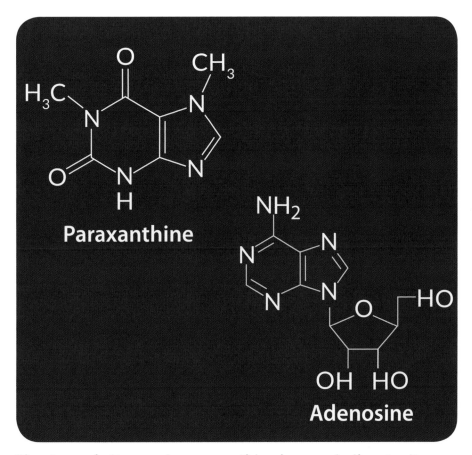

The rings of nitrogen in paraxanthine have a similar structure to those of adenosine.

makes people seek out things that make them feel happy. Caffeine lets dopamine stay in the body for a longer period of time than normal. So people keep searching for things that make them feel good. Illegal stimulants such as cocaine do the same thing. But they are much stronger than caffeine.

HEADACHE MEDICINE

Adenosine widens the blood vessels in the brain. Caffeine blocks this process. Blood vessels in the brain often enlarge before a headache. Caffeine makes the vessels narrow. This can help the headache go away. That is why caffeine is a common ingredient in headache medications.

HALF-LIFE

Scientists measure the amount of time that caffeine remains in the body. They use its half-life to do this. Half-life is the time it takes for a substance in the body to decrease by half. Different substances decrease at different rates. In a healthy adult, caffeine's half-life is 5.7 hours. An adult may have 100 milligrams of caffeine. In 5.7 hours, 50 milligrams will still be in the person's system. In another 5.7 hours, 25 milligrams will still be in the person's system.

Some people are more sensitive to caffeine. This can affect how efficiently their bodies process caffeine. It influences how caffeine affects them. The liver uses a certain enzyme to break down caffeine. Enzymes are proteins. They help with chemical reactions in the body. These reactions include breaking down food into things the body can use. Some people have a large amount of the liver enzyme. These people will break down caffeine quickly. They may not feel many of its effects. Other people have less of this enzyme. They will break down caffeine more slowly. They will feel the effects for a longer period of time.

People who drink a lot of caffeine

COFFEE IN THE UNITED STATES

Coffee did not become a popular drink in the United States until 1773. The British were heavily taxing tea shipped to the American colonies. Many people stopped drinking tea. They were protesting the taxes. They drank coffee instead. During the American Civil War (1861–1865), soldiers also drank coffee. The government provided each soldier with 36 pounds (16 kg) of coffee a year. Soldiers wanted the boost of energy that came from the caffeine. In soldiers' diaries, the word *coffee* is written more often than *war, bullet, cannon, slavery, mother,* or *Lincoln*.

may develop a tolerance to it. This means the body becomes less responsive to caffeine's effects. The first time people drink caffeine, they have no tolerance to it. The body treats it as a foreign substance. This is also the case if they have not had caffeine for a long time. But if people keep drinking the same amount of caffeine every day, the effects will fade. They won't get as much energy. The brain quickly develops more adenosine receptors to compensate for those caffeine blocks. Tolerance can happen in as few as one to four days of drinking the same amount of caffeine. The only way to avoid developing a caffeine tolerance is to drink it infrequently. Don't drink it every day. There are other reasons to limit caffeine too.

People quickly build up tolerance for caffeine. They need to consume more to get the same effect it had at first.

TAURYNĄ+ŻEŃSZEŃ
Pij schłodzony.
Napój gazowany.
ZAWIERA TAURYNĘ I KOFEIN
ENERGY
Red Bull
ENERGY DRINK
Ożywia ciało i umysł.
by
ACAI
Pij schłodzony

HOW MUCH IS TOO MUCH?

Many people rely on caffeine to help them wake up in the morning. Caffeine is the most popular mood-changing drug in the world. The National Coffee Association did a survey in 2018. It reported that 64 percent of Americans 18 and older have at least one cup of coffee a day. Ninety percent of people in the world have at least one meal or beverage with caffeine in it every day.

The suggested limit of caffeine for healthy adults is 400 milligrams a day, or about four cups of brewed coffee. The American Academy of Pediatrics suggests that teens ages 12 to 18

Tea is a popular caffeinated drink around the world. It is made from the leaves of the tea plant.

have no more than 100 milligrams of caffeine a day. That is the same as one small cup of coffee, one to two cups of tea, or two to three cans of soda. Kids under 12 should not have caffeine. But 73 percent of kids under 12 have caffeine every day.

THE SIDE EFFECTS

Most people around the world consume caffeine. But too much caffeine causes side effects. Side effects can include headaches, nausea, restlessness, and anxiety. Caffeine is also addictive. People who suddenly stop drinking their usual amounts of caffeine experience withdrawal symptoms. Symptoms include headaches and tiredness. Some people drink more than 32 ounces

People going through caffeine withdrawal may have trouble sleeping at night.

(1 L) of coffee every day. That's more than four cups of coffee a day, or more than 400 milligrams of caffeine. The symptoms of too much caffeine include severe headaches and insomnia (an inability to get enough sleep on a regular basis). They might feel nervous, irritable, or restless. They could have an upset stomach, fast heartbeat, and shakiness. For them, the withdrawal side effects can be worse.

Researchers are uncertain about caffeine's effects on some conditions. These include depression, pregnancy, diabetes, high blood pressure, and heart disease. So far, there is no conclusive data on how caffeine affects these conditions, good or bad.

CAFFEINE VERSUS MEDICINES

Caffeine can make medications less effective. It can cause bad side effects. If taken along with the stimulant ephedrine, it can damage the heart. Some antibiotics and other medications can slow the body's ability to break down caffeine. This causes the same side effects as drinking too much caffeine. Caffeine can slow the body's ability to break down some drugs. This might increase the risk of side effects from those drugs. Some medications that treat depression have stimulants. Combining these with caffeine can cause too much stimulation. People should always check with their doctors about drinking caffeine when they are given a new medication.

THE TRUTH ABOUT ENERGY DRINKS

Energy drinks usually have a lot of caffeine. Some have more than 500 milligrams of caffeine per bottle

TYPICAL CAFFEINE LEVELS IN POPULAR PRODUCTS

This graph shows the amount of caffeine in the commonly consumed amount of each drink or food. It is important for people to limit the amount of caffeine they consume. To do this, they need to know how much caffeine is in different products. What do you notice about caffeine levels? What do drinks with the highest levels of caffeine have in common?

or can. That is as much as 14 cans of soda. Energy shots are small bottles of concentrated caffeine and other ingredients. Energy shots can have between 100 and 500 milligrams of caffeine. Meanwhile, an eight-ounce (240-mL) cup of regular coffee has about 90 milligrams

ENERGY OVERDOSE

Energy drinks have a lot of caffeine. But an average adult male would have to drink approximately 149 cans of a caffeinated energy drink to get a lethal dose. He would most likely begin vomiting before he could actually drink enough to be deadly. However, a very small amount of pure caffeine powder can easily be deadly. One tablespoon, or about 10 grams, is a lethal dose for an adult. A single teaspoon of the powder is equal to up to 25 cups of coffee.

of caffeine. A 12-ounce (355-mL) can of soda contains 35 to 45 milligrams. An eight-ounce (240-mL) cup of tea has 14 to 60 milligrams.

The American Academy of Pediatrics says that children should not have energy drinks. Adults with heart problems or caffeine intolerance should not drink them either. Caffeine has side effects. But there are also benefits to consuming a moderate amount of caffeine.

STRAIGHT TO THE
SOURCE

The American Academy of Pediatrics explains the difference between energy drinks and sports drinks:

> *Sports drinks are flavored beverages that often contain carbohydrates, minerals, electrolytes (e.g., sodium, potassium, calcium, magnesium), and sometimes vitamins or other nutrients. . . . Energy drinks typically contain stimulants, such as caffeine and guarana. . . .*
>
> *For the average child engaged in routine physical activity, the use of sports drinks in place of water on the sports field or in the school lunchroom is generally unnecessary. Stimulant-containing energy drinks have no place in the diets of children or adolescents.*

Source: "Clinical Report—Sports Drinks and Energy Drinks for Children and Adolescents." *American Academy of Pediatrics*. American Academy of Pediatrics, 2011. Web. Accessed October 5, 2018.

Consider Your Audience

Review this passage closely. Consider how you would adapt it for a different audience, such as your parents or friends. Write a blog post conveying this same information for the new audience. How does your new approach differ from the original text, and why?

IT'S NOT ALL BAD NEWS

Caffeine has some good effects and uses. Most people know that it makes them more alert. It gives them more energy. But it can have other health benefits as well.

POSSIBLE POSITIVES

Researchers do not yet have a lot of data on caffeine's good effects. But there are some things that it seems to help with. Drinking three cups of coffee a day may reduce the chances of getting some cancers. It can also help decrease the risk of getting Parkinson's disease. This disease causes people to lose control of their muscles over time. Caffeine may even reduce

Many medications, including some from the 1950s, have used caffeine.

the chances of getting type 2 diabetes. This disease keeps the body from balancing sugar levels. Some elderly people have problems with dizziness and low blood pressure after eating. Caffeine may increase their blood pressure. It may help prevent dizziness.

Studies also show that caffeine might help improve memory. It may reduce the risk of getting Alzheimer's disease. This disease causes memory loss. Experiments suggest that caffeine may prevent skin cancer. It could protect against cataracts in the eyes. It may also help with asthma. This is because caffeine is similar to the drug used to open up airways during asthma attacks. However, little is known about why caffeine may help in these cases. And all of these results require more study before they can be accepted as true.

CAFFEINE MYTHS

There are many myths about caffeine. One is that caffeine is not safe. Caffeine is safe as long as it is used in moderation. It also needs to be used with

CAFFEINE'S EFFECT ON THE BODY

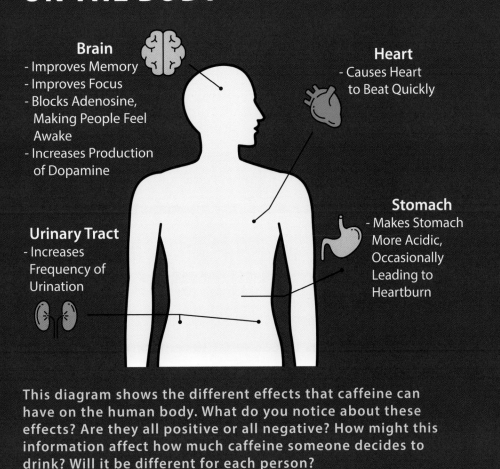

Brain
- Improves Memory
- Improves Focus
- Blocks Adenosine, Making People Feel Awake
- Increases Production of Dopamine

Heart
- Causes Heart to Beat Quickly

Stomach
- Makes Stomach More Acidic, Occasionally Leading to Heartburn

Urinary Tract
- Increases Frequency of Urination

This diagram shows the different effects that caffeine can have on the human body. What do you notice about these effects? Are they all positive or all negative? How might this information affect how much caffeine someone decides to drink? Will it be different for each person?

common sense. The US Food and Drug Administration has labeled it as a substance that is generally recognized as safe. Some people believe that caffeine causes heart problems. There is no evidence of this.

However, it can be a problem for people who have existing heart conditions.

> ## NATURE'S PESTICIDE
>
> **In plants, caffeine acts as a natural pesticide. It paralyzes and kills insects that try to feed on plants treated with it. Caffeine also keeps seeds from sprouting near the plant. This limits the number of plants that could compete for resources.**

Another myth is that caffeine is bad for pregnant women or women trying to become pregnant. There is no scientific link between caffeine and problems with pregnancy. Several major studies show no link to birth defects or difficulties in getting pregnant. But doctors do recommend that pregnant and nursing women limit how much caffeine they drink to 200 milligrams a day or less. An additional myth is that caffeine helps with weight loss. So far, there is no evidence to prove this.

THE BOTTOM LINE

Caffeine is fine for most people as long as they don't have too much. The tricky part is knowing which foods contain it. Foods such as gum, jelly beans, gummy bears, chips, waffles, syrup, marshmallows, sunflower seeds, and other snacks may have caffeine. Any food with a label that mentions energy is a possible caffeine source.

The best way to control caffeine intake is to drink decaffeinated sodas and coffee. Soda can be decaffeinated simply by not adding caffeine to the drink. Decaffeinated coffee can be made using

WIRED WAFFLES

Many manufacturers are taking part in the craze for foods that give people energy. They add caffeine to things that usually wouldn't have it. Alert gum has caffeine. Cracker Jack'd is a new version of the famous snack Cracker Jack. One serving contains as much caffeine as a cup of coffee. Perky Jerky is beef jerky with caffeine. Wired Waffles's waffles and syrup have added caffeine. Morning Spark instant oatmeal has 60 milligrams of caffeine.

Some soda labels will note if a product is free of caffeine.

coffee beans that have been soaked and treated with chemicals. This removes most of the natural caffeine in them. Another process for decaffeinating coffee beans involves soaking them in water. However, even decaffeinated coffee contains some caffeine. Avoid energy drinks and energy shots. Drink water instead.

Caffeine intake can be reduced gradually. Have a smaller cup of coffee or one less can of soda each day. Caffeinated tea can be replaced with noncaffeinated herbal teas. Don't have caffeine at least five hours before bedtime.

Caffeine can be helpful. It can also be harmful. Some people may not know how much they get every day. But by balancing caffeine intake, people can improve their health and sleep quality without giving up a piece of chocolate or cup of coffee.

FURTHER EVIDENCE

Chapter Five talks about some of the health benefits of caffeine. What is the main point? What evidence is used to support that point? Now visit the website below. Find a quote from the article that supports the chapter's main point. Does it support a piece of evidence found in the chapter, or does it offer new evidence?

HEALTH BENEFITS AND RISKS ASSOCIATED WITH CAFFEINE

abdocorelibrary.com/caffeine

FAST FACTS

- Caffeine is a stimulant that affects the brain and central nervous system.

- Caffeine is the most commonly used stimulant in the world.

- Caffeine is found in coffee, tea, chocolate, energy drinks, and some sodas.

- Caffeine is often an added ingredient in foods that are marketed as giving people energy.

- Caffeine increases the level of dopamine in the brain. This causes people to search for things that make them happy.

- Caffeine causes sleeplessness.

- Caffeine is often used as a supplement to increase concentration.

- Side effects of too much caffeine include jitteriness, wakefulness, increased heart rate, headaches, and anxiety.

- Energy drinks often contain high amounts of caffeine.

- The recommended daily amount of caffeine for adults is 400 milligrams or less, or about four cups of brewed coffee.

- There is no known safe amount of caffeine for kids under 12 years old.

STOP AND THINK

Tell the Tale

Chapter One of this book gives an example of a boy who ends up drinking far more caffeine than he realizes and what happens to him as a result. Write a story about a similar circumstance that you or one of your friends has experienced after having too many caffeinated beverages or foods.

Surprise Me

Chapter Two discusses different foods and drinks with caffeine in them. After reading this book, what two or three facts about caffeine levels in food and drinks did you find most surprising? Write a few sentences about each fact. Why did you find each fact surprising?

Another View

This book talks about caffeine and how doctors and nutritionists generally do not recommend it for kids and teens. As you know, every source is different. Ask a librarian or another adult to help you find another source about

this issue. Write a short essay comparing and contrasting the new source's point of view with that of this book's author. What is the point of view of each author? How are they similar and why? How are they different and why?

You Are There

This book discusses the effects of caffeine on kids and adults. Imagine that, effective immediately, your parents decide that no one in your household will have anything caffeinated anymore. Write a journal about what happens to everyone as they stop drinking their regular amounts of caffeine. Include a week's worth of entries. What drinks and foods do you miss? Be sure to use a lot of detail about how everyone is feeling during the process of caffeine withdrawal.

GLOSSARY

electrolyte
a positively or negatively charged particle such as a sodium molecule that controls how nutrients flow around the body

extract
a concentrated form of a substance that still contains the active ingredient

liver
a large organ that cleans your blood, helps digest food, and stores sugar as glycogen

membrane
a thin layer of tissue that separates two parts of a human or animal body

molecule
the smallest unit of a chemical compound

nutrient
something in food that helps people, animals, and plants live and grow

pesticide
a substance that repels or kills unwanted insects and other pests

receptor
a specialized cell or group of nerve endings that responds to changes and sends signals to the body to behave a certain way

stimulate
to cause to become active

supplement
something, such as vitamins, that are added to the diet for a specific purpose

ONLINE
RESOURCES

To learn more about your body on caffeine, visit our free resource websites below.

Visit **abdocorelibrary.com** or scan this QR code for free Common Core resources for teachers and students, including vetted activities, multimedia, and booklinks, for deeper subject comprehension.

Visit **abdobooklinks.com** or scan this QR code for free additional online weblinks for further learning. These links are routinely monitored and updated to provide the most current information available.

LEARN
MORE

Francis, Amy, ed. *Caffeine*. Farmington Hills, MI: Greenhaven Press, 2016. Print.

Petersen, Christine. *Caffeine and Energy Drinks*. New York: Cavendish Square, 2014. Print.

INDEX

About the Author

Marcia Amidon Lusted has written more than 160 books and 600 magazine articles for young readers. She is also an editor and a musician. She drinks coffee every day, but she tries not to drink too much.